CLASSIC EXPERIENCE ENCORES

FOR EASY PIANO

A further selection of EASY-TO-PLAY arrangements for piano of themes from some of the world's most popular classics, as featured in the hugely successful recording compilations.

Arranged by Jerry Lanning

With acknowledgement to EMI Records and Garden Studio for permission to use the cover illustrations

Cover Illustrations: Simon Williams (Garden Studio)
Music Setting: Spartan Press Music Publishers Ltd.
Cover Design: Collyer Graphics
Printers: Halstan
Copyright: 1994 Middle Eight Music Ltd.
Published by: Cramer Music Ltd.
23 Garrick Street, London WC2E 9AX

CONTENTS

ANVIL CHORUS

from *Il Trovatore*

Allegro

Giuseppe Verdi

C.M. Ltd. 2163

4

ARRIVAL OF
THE QUEEN OF SHEBA

from *Solomon*

Allegro

George Frideric Handel

C.M. Ltd. 2163

BERCEUSE

from the *Dolly Suite*

Allegretto moderato

Gabriel Fauré

C.M. Ltd. 2163

ITALIAN SYMPHONY

First Movement

Allegro vivace

Felix Mendelssohn

C.M. Ltd. 2163

MONTAGUES AND CAPULETS

from *Romeo and Juliet*

Allegro pesante

Serge Prokofiev

C.M. Ltd. 2163

col 8va ad lib. _

col 8va ad lib. _ _ _ _ _ _ _ _ _ _ _ _ _ _ _ _ _

LA DONNA È MOBILE

from *Rigoletto*

Allegretto

Giuseppe Verdi

C.M. Ltd. 2163

MOONLIGHT SONATA

First Movement

Adagio sostenuto

Ludwig van Beethoven

C.M. Ltd. 2163

Themes from
PETER AND THE WOLF

Serge Prokofiev

C.M. Ltd. 2163

NOCTURNE

from *String Quartet No. 2*

Andante

Alexander Borodin

C.M. Ltd. 2163

PIANO CONCERTO IN A MINOR

First Movement

Allegro molto moderato

Edvard Grieg

C.M. Ltd. 2163

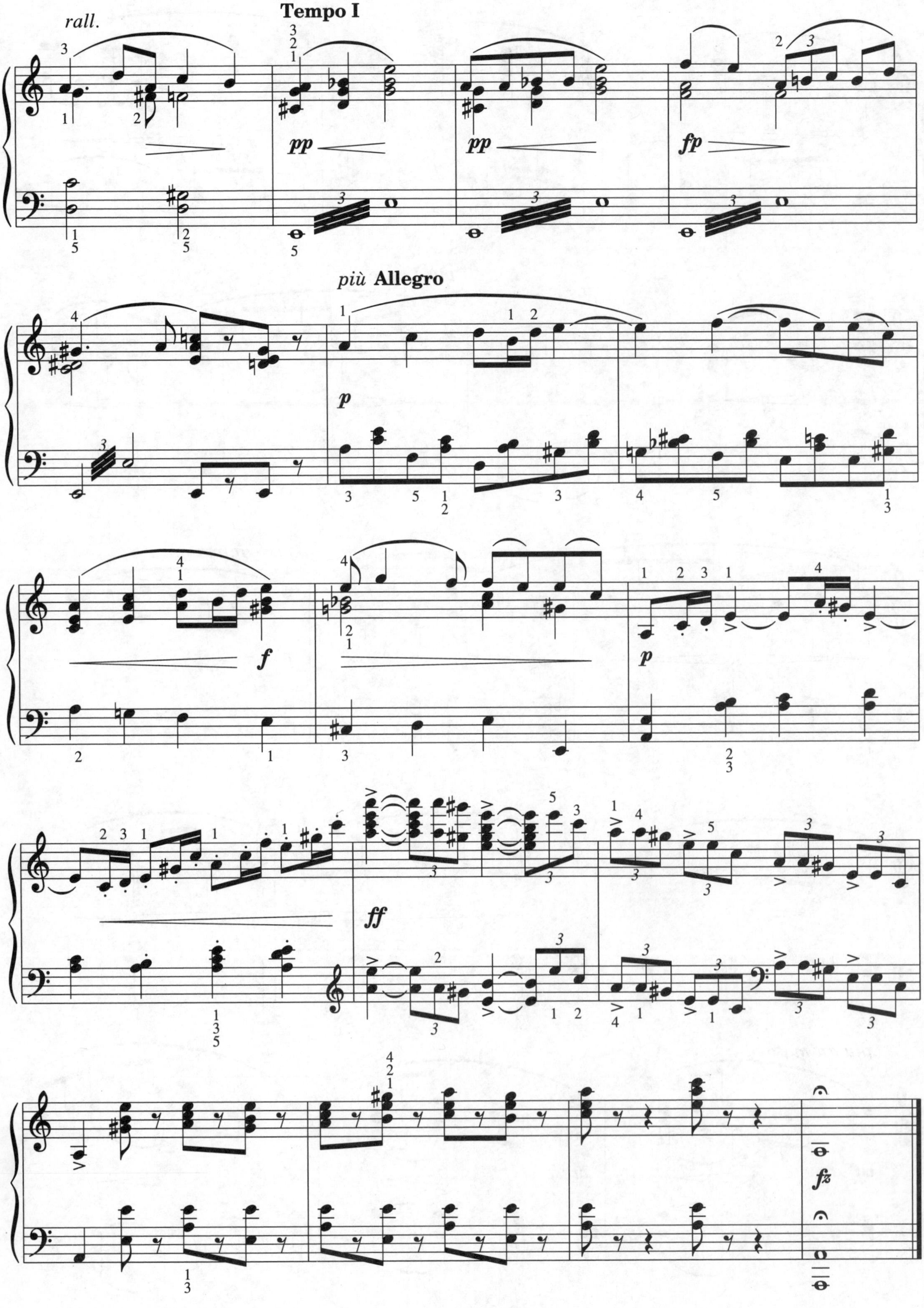
rall.
Tempo I
pp
pp
fp
più Allegro
p
f
p
ff
fz

PIZZICATO POLKA

from *Sylvia*

Allegretto

Leo Delibes

C.M. Ltd. 2164

RUSSIAN DANCE

from *The Nutcracker*

Molto vivace

Peter Ilich Tchaikovsky

C.M. Ltd. 2163

THE SKATERS' WALTZ

Valse moderato

Emil Waldteufel

C.M. Ltd. 2163

RECUERDOS DE LA ALHAMBRA

Andante

Francisco Tarrega

C.M. Ltd. 2163

THE SWAN

from *The Carnival of the Animals*

Andantino grazioso

Camille Saint-Saëns

C.M. Ltd. 2163

TRIUMPHAL MARCH

from *Aida*

Allegro maestoso

Giuseppe Verdi

C.M. Ltd. 2163

WALTZ

from *Coppélia*

Tempo di Valse

Leo Delibes

C.M. Ltd. 2163